Pen Pals

by Michael Rose Ramirez

Illustrated by Higgins Bond

Ray,

It is fall here.

I am raking leaves!

Ann

Ray Rivera
304 Palm Drive
Miami, Florida
33107

Ann,

It is fall here, too.

I'm running on the beach!

Ray

Ann Dixon
14 Oak Lane
Rutland, Vermont
05702

Ray,

It is winter here.

I am building a big snowman!

Ann

Ray Rivera
304 Palm Drive
Miami, Florida
33107

Ann,

It is winter here, too.

I'm sailing on my boat!

Ray

Ann Dixon
14 Oak Lane
Rutland, Vermont
05702

Ray,

It is spring here.

I am planting flowers!

Ann

Ray Rivera
304 Palm Drive
Miami, Florida
33107

Ann,

It is spring here, too.

I'm building a big sandcastle!

Ray

Ann Dixon
14 Oak Lane
Rutland, Vermont
05702

Ray,

It is summer here.

I am swimming in the lake!

Ann

Ray Rivera
304 Palm Drive
Miami, Florida
33107